Let's Go!

Subway Rides

By Pamela Walker

Children's Press
A Division of Grolier Publishing
New York / London / Hong Kong / Sydney
Danbury, Connecticut

Photo Credits: Cover and all photos by Thaddeus Harden

Contributing Editors: Mark Beyer and Eliza Berkowitz
Book Design: MaryJane Wojciechowski

Visit Children's Press on the Internet at:
http://publishing.grolier.com

Library of Congress Cataloging-in-Publication Data

Walker, Pamela, 1958-
   Subway rides / by Pamela Walker.
      p. cm. — (Let's go)
   Includes bibliographical references and index.
   Summary: Photographs and simple text describe a subway ride, including walking
down into the station, going through the turnstile, waiting for the train, riding inside the
crowded car, and waving to the conductor after exiting.
   ISBN 0-516-23103-0 (lib. bdg.) — ISBN 0-516-23028-X (pbk.)
   1. Subways—United States—Juvenile literature. [1. Subways.] I. Title. II. Series.

HE4451.W83 2000
388.4'28'0973—dc21

                                                                              00-025450

Contents

My dad takes me to school every morning on the **subway**.

There is a sign for the subway.

The subway **station** is **underground**.

Astor Place Station
Downtown & The Bronx only   6

5

We use **tokens** to pay for our rides.

I put the token in the slot.

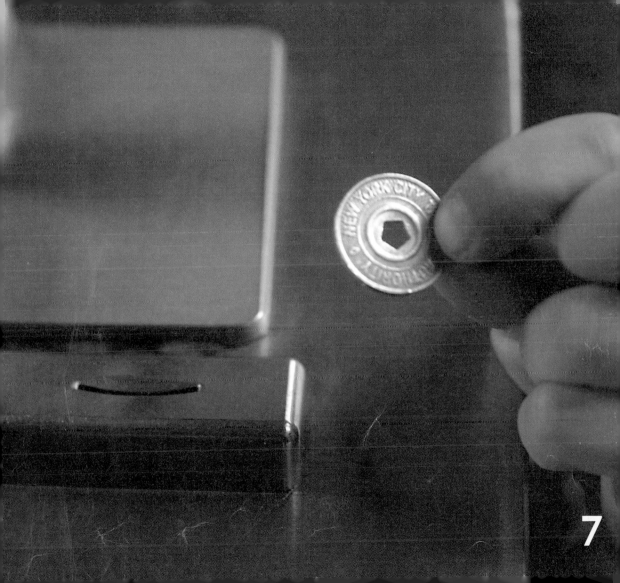

7

Other people ride the subway, too.

I stand behind the yellow line where it's safe.

9

Here comes the subway.

I can see the **brakeman**.

He sits in the first car.

6 Pelham Bay Park

11

The subway stops and the doors open.

We get on the subway.

13

There are a lot of people on the subway.

Some people like to sit while riding the subway.

We like to stand and hold onto a pole.

15

The subway stops at every station.

People get on and off at every stop.

9167

New York City Subway

9166

17

The **conductor** looks out the window.

She checks to make sure everyone is inside.

9167

New York City Subway

23

23

The subway stops at another station.

This is our stop.

The doors open and we get off.

After school, my dad will take me home on the subway.

21

New Words

brakeman (**brayk**-man) the person who drives the train

conductor (kun-**duk**-ter) the person who controls the subway doors

station (**stay**-shun) the building where trains stop

subway (**sub**-way) the train

tokens (**toh**-kins) pieces of metal shaped like coins

underground (**uhn**-der-**ground**) below the ground

To Find Out More

Books

Friday's Journey
by Ken Rush
Orchard Books

Subways
by Allison Lassleur
Capstone Press

Underground Train
by Mary Quattlebaum
Bantam Doubleday Dell Books for Young Readers

Web Sites
Metropolitan Transportation Authority
http://www.mta.nyc.ny.us
This is the official site of the Metropolitan Transportation Authority. It has a lot of facts about the public transportation system in New York City.

www.nycsubway.org
http://www.nycsubway.org
Here you can learn the history of the New York City subway system. This site has information about how the subway works and has a lot of pictures.

Index

About the Author
Pamela Walker lives in Brooklyn, New York. She takes a train to work every day, but enjoys all forms of transportation.

Reading Consultants
Kris Flynn, Coordinator, Small School District Literacy, The San Diego County Office of Education

Shelly Forys, Certified Reading Recovery Specialist, W.J. Zahnow Elementary School, Waterloo, IL

Peggy McNamara, Professor, Bank Street College of Education, Reading and Literacy Program